FASHION DESIGN

MODEENTWÜRFE
DISEÑOS DE LA MODA
DESIGN DI MODA
CRÉATIONS DE MODE

1850-1895

FASHION DESIGN

MODEENTWÜRFE
DISEÑOS DE LA MODA
DESIGN DI MODA
CRÉATIONS DE MODE

1850-1895

By Design Press
New York
an imprint of
Quite Specific Media Group Ltd.

Copyright for this edition © 1997 The Pepin Press B/V
Copyright introduction 'Fashion Design 1850-1895' © 1997 The Pepin Press B/V

Edited and produced by Dorine van den Beukel

First published in 1997 by
The Pepin Press B/V
POB 10349, 1001 EH Amsterdam
The Netherlands
Tel (+) 31 20 4202021, Fax (+) 31 20 4201152
email: pepin@euronet.nl

Published in the USA by
By Design Press
an imprint of
Quite Specific Media Group Ltd.
260 Fifth Avenue, Suite 703
New York, NY 10001

(212) 725-5377 voice, (212) 725-8506 fax
email: info@quitespecificmedia.com

Other Quite Specific Media Group Ltd. imprints:

Drama Publishers
Costume & Fashion Press
EntertainmentPro
Jade Rabbit

For other QSM titles online:
http://www.quitespecificmedia.com

ISBN 0-89676-223-8

Printed in Singapore

Fashion Design 1850-1895

This Pepin Press Design book contains a large collection of fashion drawings dating from the years 1850-1895. As with other volumes in these series, the intention of this book is not to provide a complete survey of fashion in the second half of the nineteenth century, but to offer a vast selection of high-quality reproductions as reference material and a source of inspiration for designers. It not only contains illustrations of standard day-to-day clothing, but also detailed pictures of formal evening dress, shoes, bags, parasols, wedding dresses, knitwear, children's clothing, lace, pompons, sportswear, bow ties and more.

Around 1850, women wore dresses which were tightly corsetted at the waist, with huge skirts supported by cages or crinolines. In the 1860's dresses were flattened at the front and extended more at the back to make a train, which was supported by a bustle. Later, the bustle disappeared and the so called princesse-line came into fashion: slim dresses without a waist seam, with a longer bodice, and adorned with lots of draperies, ribbons, trimmings and puffs. During the 1880's the bustle reappeared, this time in a more exaggerated shape than before; skirts almost stood out horizontally at the back. Just before the turn of the century, around 1895, the fashion changed again with dresses displaying a different silhouette: a full bust, tiny waist, wide skirts and huge sleeves.

Evening dress resembled everyday clothing, but as a rule made use of more delicate and precious materials. Evening gowns were more heavily ornamented, with lower cuts and shorter sleeves. Until the 1880's, aprons were worn as informal dress or evening dress, in the latter case embellished with lace and ribbons. Hereafter, aprons were only worn by domestic servants. Wedding dresses were made of white silk or silk with lace. Mourning dress was black, or sometimes dark brown, and was worn with matching accessories: veils, hats, gloves, handkerchiefs and jewellery.

Sportswear first appeared in the nineteenth century. Around 1850, the first bathing costumes were created. Initially they were made in one-piece, later becoming a tunic worn over a pair of trousers. Because of the inconvenience of normal dresses with their crinolines or bustles, special walking dresses were designed, which were also used for playing tennis. Riding costumes mostly comprised a long skirt with a small jacket. Later, shorter skirts with knickerbockers underneath became fashionable for cycling and shooting.

Capes, mantles, shawls, mantlets, half-shawls, tippets, short shoulder capes, pardessus, pelisses or carriage dresses, and paletots were all popular outdoor clothing. The dolman, a three-quarter length cape with a generous cut to accommodate a dress with a bustle, was fashionable in the 1870's and 1880's. Fur coats became fashionable in the 1890's.

Late nineteenth-century underwear includes a whole variety of different garments: corsets, bustles, crinolines, chemises, drawers, camisoles, petticoats, négligées and nightdresses. Tight corsets were used to reduce the waistline, and were sometimes worn so tight as to cause broken ribs. Crinolines, the cages supporting the skirts and worn underneath layers of petticoats, were made with horsehair and crin (linen), on whalebone, steel or cane hoops.

Accessories, such as shoes, gloves, muffs, bags, and parasols often matched the dresses with which they were worn, and thus followed the prevailing fashions.

Modeentwürfe 1850-1895

Dieser Band der Pepin Press Design-Buch-Reihe enthält eine große Auswahl Modezeichnungen aus den Jahren 1850 bis 1895. Wie die anderen Bände in dieser Reihe wird nicht beabsichtigt, eine komplette Übersicht über die Mode des 19. Jahrhunderts zu geben, vielmehr sind eine Vielzahl Reproduktionen in hoher Qualität abgebildet, die Designern als Vorlage und Inspirationsquelle dienen: Beispiele der Alltagsmode, detaillierte Abbildungen der Abendmode, Schuhe, Handtaschen, Schirme, Hochzeitskleider, Strickwaren, Kindermode, Spitzen, Falten, Quasten, Sportmode, Schleifen und vieles mehr.

Um 1850 trugen Frauen Kleider mit eng anliegenden Taillen und weiten Röcken, die mit Reifröcken und Krinolinen gestützt werden mußten. In den 60er Jahren wurden die Kleider vorne flacher, hinten jedoch zu einer Schleppe verlängert, die von einer Turnüre unterstützt wurde. Später verschwand die Turnüre und die sogenannte Prinzeß-Linie kam in Mode: schmale Kleider ohne Taillennaht, mit längerem Mieder und mit vielen Draperien, Bändern, Borten und Bäuschen verziert. In den 80er Jahren wurden Turnüre wieder populär und zwar in einer noch extremeren Form als zuvor. Die Röcke standen hinten nahezu horizontal ab. Kurz vor der Jahrhundertwende, um 1895, änderte sich die Mode wieder; die Kleider zeigten eine andere Silhouette mit vollem Busen, Wespentaille, weiten Röcken und ausgeprägten Ärmeln.

Das Abendkleid ähnelte dem Tageskleid, jedoch wurden in der Regel kostbarere und feinere Materialien verwendet. Die Abendkleider waren besonders verziert, tiefer ausgeschnitten und hatten kürzere Ärmel. Bis etwa 1880 trug man einfache Schürzen zum zwanglosen Kleid und Schürzen mit Spitzen und Bänder zum Abendkleid. Danach wurden Schürzen nur noch vom Hauspersonal getragen. Hochzeitskleider waren aus weißer Seide oder Seide mit Spitze. Trauerkleider, in Schwarz oder Dunkelbraun, wurden mit passenden Accessoires kombiniert: Schleier, Hüte, Handschuhe, Taschentücher und Schmuck.

Sportmode kam zum ersten Mal im 19. Jahrhundert auf. Um 1850 gab es die ersten Badeanzüge; anfänglich als ganzteiliges Kostüm, später als Tunika, die über ein Paar Hosen getragen werden konnte. Da Kleider mit Krinolinen und Turnüren unbequem waren, wurden besondere Ausgehkleider entworfen, die man auch zum Tennis spielen trug. Reitkostüme bestanden hauptsächlich aus einem langen Rock mit schmaler Jacke. Zum Radfahren oder für die Jagd kamen später kürzere Röcke in Mode, die über Knickerbockers getragen wurden.

Capes, Umhänge, Schals, Mäntel, Tücher, Pelerinen, kurze Schultercapes, Pardessus, lange Mäntel oder Kutschermäntel und Paletots waren beliebte Kleidung für draußen. Der Dolman, ein dreiviertellanger Umhang, der auch über Kleider mit Turnüre getragen werden konnte, war in den 70er und 80er Jahren modern. Pelzmäntel wurden in den 90er Jahren populär.

Die Unterwäsche des späten 19. Jahrhunderts bestand aus vielen Einzelstücken: Korsetts, Turnüren, Krinolinen, Hemdchen, Schlüpfer, Hemdhosen, Petticoats, Négligés und Nachthemden. Enge Korsetts wurden getragen, um eine Wespentaille zu erreichen, was manchmal sogar zu gebrochenen Rippen führte. Krinolinen, Reifröcke aus Roßhaar und Roßhaargewebe, Fischbein, Korsettstäbchen oder Peddigrohrreifen, wurden zur Stützung der Röcke unter einer Vielzahl von Petticoats getragen.

Accessoires wie Schuhe, Handschuhe, Muffs, Taschen und Schirme waren meist passend zu den Kleidern, mit denen sie kombiniert wurden und änderten sich mit der jeweiligen Moderichtung.

Créations de Mode 1850-1895

Ce livre de la série Design de Pepin Press contient une large collection de dessins de mode des années 1850-1895. Comme pour les autres volumes de ces séries, l'intention de ce livre n'est pas de fournir une étude complète de la mode au cours de la seconde moitié du dix-neuvième siècle, mais d'offrir un vaste choix de reproductions de haute qualité comme référence et source d'inspiration pour les créateurs. Ce livre regroupe non seulement des illustrations représentant les vêtements de tous les jours mais également des images détaillées de tenues de soirée, de costumes portés aux bals masqués, de chaussures, de sacs, d'ombrelles, de robes de mariée, de tricots, de tenues d'enfants, de dentelles, de plissés, de pompons, de vêtements de sport, de noeuds papillon etcetera.

Aux environs de 1850, les femmes portaient des robes étroites à la taille mais dont les jupes étaient très larges et par conséquent devaient être supportées par des cages ou des crinolines. Dans les années 1860, les robes s'applatissaient sur le devant mais s'étendaient par une traîne soutenue par une tournure dans le dos. Plus tard, la tournure disparaissait, et la ligne *Princesse* devenait à la mode: petites robes sans coutures à la taille avec un corsage plus long et ornées de beaucoup de drapés, de rubans, de passementerie et de bouillons. Vers 1880, la tournure réapparut cette foi-ci dans une forme plus extrême qu'auparavant. Les jupes étaient presque à l'horizontale dans le dos. Peu avant la fin du siècle, autour de 1895, la mode changeait encore et les robes montraient une autre silhouette avec un buste plein, une taille de guêpe, de larges jupes et d'immenses manches.

Les robes de soirée ressemblaient aux robes de jour, mais dans une coutume plus délicate et des tissus précieux étaient utilisés. Les robes de soirée étaient plus abondemment ornées, avaient des coupes plus basses et des manches plus courtes. Les tabliers étaient portés comme d'informelles robes ou robes de soirée – dans ce dernier cas améliorées de dentelles et de rubans – jusqu'en 1880. Après cela, ils étaient portés par les domestiques uniquement. Les robes de mariage étaient faites de soie blanche ou de soie avec des dentelles. Les habits de deuil étaient noirs ou parfois marron foncé et portés avec des accessoires assortis: voiles, chapeaux, gants, mouchoirs et bijoux.

Les vêtements de sport faisaient leur première apparition au dix-neuvième siècle. Autour de 1850, les premiers costumes de bain apparurent. Initialement, un costume d'une pièce, plus tard une tunique portée sur un pantalon. À cause de l'inconvénience des robes à crinolines ou à tournures, des robes de marche furent créées qui furent également utilisées pour jouer au tennis. Les costumes d'équitation consistaient en une longue jupe et une courte veste. Plus tard, des jupes plus courtes avec des shorts dessous devenaient à la mode pour le cyclisme et la chasse.

Capes, mantes, châles, étoles, pardessus, pelisses, tenues d'équipage, paletots tous étaient populaires comme étant des tenues d'extérieur. Les manteaux de fourrure devinrent à la mode dans les années 1890.

Les sous-vêtements de la fin du dix-neuvième siècle montrent un grand nombre de variétés: corsets, tournures, crinolines, chemises, culottes, camisoles, jupons, négligés et robes de nuit. D'étroits corsets étaient portés pour obtenir une taille fine et causaient parfois des fractures de côtes. Les crinolines, les cages supportant les jupes et portées sous de nombreux jupons, étaient faites de poils de chevaux et de crin, d'os de baleine, de cerceaux de canne ou d'acier.

Les accessoires tels que les chaussures, les gants, les manchons, les sacs et les ombrelles étaient souvent assortis aux robes avec lesquels ils étaient portés et changeaient avec les styles dominants de la mode.

Design di Moda 1850-1895

Questo libro della Pepin Press Design Series, contiene un'ampia collezione di disegni che illus-
trano la moda degli anni che vanno dal 1850 al 1895. Anche questo volume, come tutti gli altri
della stessa serie, non intende offrire un panorama completo della moda della seconda metà
dell'Ottocento, ma si propone piuttosto di presentare un'ampia collezione di riproduzioni di alta
qualità, che servano di riferimento e di ispirazione agli stilisti. Vi si trovano immagini
dell'abbigliamento di tutti i giorni, ma anche illustrazioni ricche di dettagli di abiti da sera, abiti
portati alle sciarade, scarpe, borse, ombrelli, abiti da sposa, maglieria, abbigliamento per bam-
bini, pizzi, pieghe, nappe, abbigliamento sportivo, farfalline, eccetera.

Intorno al 1850 le donne portano abiti con la vita stretta e gonne molto ampie, che richiedono il
sostegno di armature o crinoline. Negli anni '60 invece le gonne cadono in verticale sul davanti
e formano uno strascico all'indietro, sostenute da un cuscinetto. Più tardi il cuscinetto sparisce,
con l'affermarsi della linea Princesse, con abiti snelli, in un solo pezzo, senza cucitura alla vita,
con un corpino allungato e ornati da una quantità di drappeggi, nastri, merletti e sbuffi. Negli
anni '80 torna in auge il cuscinetto – noto anche come *Cul de Paris* – affermandosi in forme più
pronunciate che mai, tanto che le gonne si prolungano all'indietro quasi orizzontali. Proprio
nello scorcio del secolo, intorno al 1895, la moda cambia di nuovo e gli abiti si impostano su
una silhouette nuova, con petto ampio e pronunciato e vita stretta, gonne ampie e maniche
abbondanti.

L'abbigliamento da sera non era molto differente da quello portato di giorno, ma di regola veni-
va realizzato con materiali più fini e preziosi. Gli abiti da sera avevano un ornamento più ricco,
scollature più basse e maniche più corte. I grembiuli si portavano tanto sugli abiti semplici
quanto – abbelliti da pizzi e nastri – su quelli da sera, fino agli anni '80, dopodiché sono rimasti
riservati al personale di servizio domestico. Gli abiti da sposa erano di seta bianca o di seta con
pizzi. Gli abiti da lutto erano di colore nero, talvolta pure marrone scuro, e si accompagnavano
con accessori intonati: velette, cappelli, guanti, fazzoletti e gioielli.

È proprio nel XIX secolo che fa la sua apparizione per la prima volta l'abbigliamento sportivo.
Intorno al 1850 vedono la luce i primi costumi da bagno. Si tratta al principio di costumi a un
pezzo, sostituiti più tardi da tunichette portate sopra un paio di calzoni. Data la scomodità degli
abiti normali, impacciati da crinoline o cuscinetti, vengono disegnati abiti da passeggio, indos-
sati anche per giocare a tennis. Le amazzoni portano generalmente una gonna lunga con una
giacca corta. Più tardi si afferma la moda di gonne più corte, con sotto calzoni alla zuava, per
andare in bicicletta o partecipare a gare di tiro.

Cappe, mantelline, scialli, mantelletti, mezzi scialli, stole, coprispalle corti, cappotti, soprabiti o
abiti da carrozza e paletot erano molto usati per indossare fuori casa. Il dolman, un soprabito a
tre quarti che si poteva indossare su un abito con Cul de Paris, era di moda negli anni '70 e '80.
La moda delle pellicce si afferma negli anni '90.

La biancheria intima degli ultimi anni dell'Ottocento mostra un gran numero di capi di abbigliamento diversi: busti, cuscinetti, crinoline, camicie, mutandoni, corpetti, sottovesti, négligé e
camicie da notte. Una vita snella la si conquistava indossando busti stretti e rigidi e la si pagava
spesso a prezzo di fratture costali. Le crinoline, quelle armature che sostenevano le gonne e si
portavano sotto un certo numero di sottovesti, erano di crine di cavallo e venivano tenute
allargate con stecche di balena e cerchi di acciaio o di canna.

Accessori quali le scarpe, i guanti, i manicotti, le borse e gli ombrelli erano spesso intonati agli
abiti a cui si accompagnavano e cambiavano secondo gli stili della moda.

Diseños de la Moda 1850-1895

Este libro de la serie de Diseño de Pepin Press contiene una amplia colección de diseños de moda de los años 1850 a 1895. Al igual que los otros volúmenes de esta serie, la intención del presente libro no es la de proporcionar un análisis exhaustivo de la moda de la segunda mitad del siglo diecinueve, sino la de ofrecer un conjunto de reproducciones de alta calidad que sirva de referencia y fuente de inspiración a los diseñadores. Contiene ilustraciones no solamente del vestir cotidiano, sino también de vestidos de noche y de fiesta, así como de zapatos, bolsos, sombrillas, vestidos de boda, géneros de punto, prendas infantiles, encajes, pliegues, borlas, prendas deportivas, corbatas de lazo, etcétera.

Alrededor de 1850, las mujeres llevaban vestidos ceñidos a la cintura con amplias faldas que necesitaban sujetar con miriñaques. En la década siguiente los vestidos se volvieron menos profusos en la parte anterior y se alargaron por detrás con una cola, para lo cual se hizo necesario el uso del polisón. Más tarde éste desapareció y se puso de moda la denominada línea principesca: vestidos estilizados no ceñidos a la cintura, de cuerpo largo y provistos de múltiples paños, cintas, adornos y borlas. Hacia 1880 reapareció el polisón, esta vez con una forma mucho más exagerada que hasta entonces, de modo que en la parte trasera las faldas quedaban casi suspendidas en horizontal. Poco antes del cambio de siglo, hacia 1895, la moda dió un nuevo giro y los vestidos adquirieron un corte muy distinto: se impusieron los grandes escotes, cinturas estrechas, faldas amplias y mangas ampulosas.

Los vestidos de noche eran similares a los de día, si bien por norma los materiales usados eran de mayor delicadeza y valor. Estos vestidos estaban provistos de numerosos ornamentos, eran más largos y de mangas más cortas. El delantal se consideró una prenda informal o parte del vestido de noche (en este último caso adornado con encajes y lazos) hasta la década de 1880; después pasó solamente a vestirla el servicio doméstico. Los vestidos de boda estaban confeccionados con seda blanca o seda con encajes. Los vestidos de luto eran de color negro o en ciertas ocasiones de color marrón oscuro, acompañados de accesorios a juego: velos, sombreros, guantes, pañuelos y joyas.

Las prendas deportivas hicieron su primera aparición en el siglo diecinueve. Hacia 1850 se elaboraron los primeros artículos de baño, que en un principio, estaban formados por una sola pieza y más tarde pasaron a constar de túnica y pantalones. Debido a la incomodidad que representaban los vestidos normales por el miriñaque o el polisón, se diseñaron vestidos especiales de paseo, que también se utilizaban para jugar a tenis. Los trajes de montar constaban en su mayoría de una falda larga con una chaqueta pequeña. Más adelante se pusieron de moda las faldas más cortas con pantalones bombachos debajo para montar en bicicleta o practicar el deporte de la caza.

Las capas, los mantos, los chales, las esclavinas, los capotillos, las capas cortas, los gabanes, las pellizas y los paletós se encontraban entre las prendas de exterior más populares. El dolmán, una capa de tres cuartos que permitía llevar vestido con polisón, estuvo muy de moda en las décadas de 1870 y 1880. Los abrigos de piel se pusieron de moda hacia 1890.

Un gran número de prendas distintas integran la ropa interior de finales del siglo diecinueve: corsés, polisones, miriñaques, camisolas, calzas, cubrecorsés, enaguas, mantos de encajes y camisones. Estaba extendido el uso del corsé ajustado, con el cual se conseguía una cintura fina y que, en ocasiones, causaba incluso rotura de costillas. El polisón, estructura que sujetaba la falda y que se llevaba bajo diversas enaguas, estaba confeccionado con crin de caballo, huesos de ballena y aros de acero o mimbre.

Los accesorios, como el calzado, los guantes, los manguitos, los bolsos y las sombrillas solían hacer juego con los vestidos a los que acompañaban y fueron cambiando al ritmo de la moda.

13

24

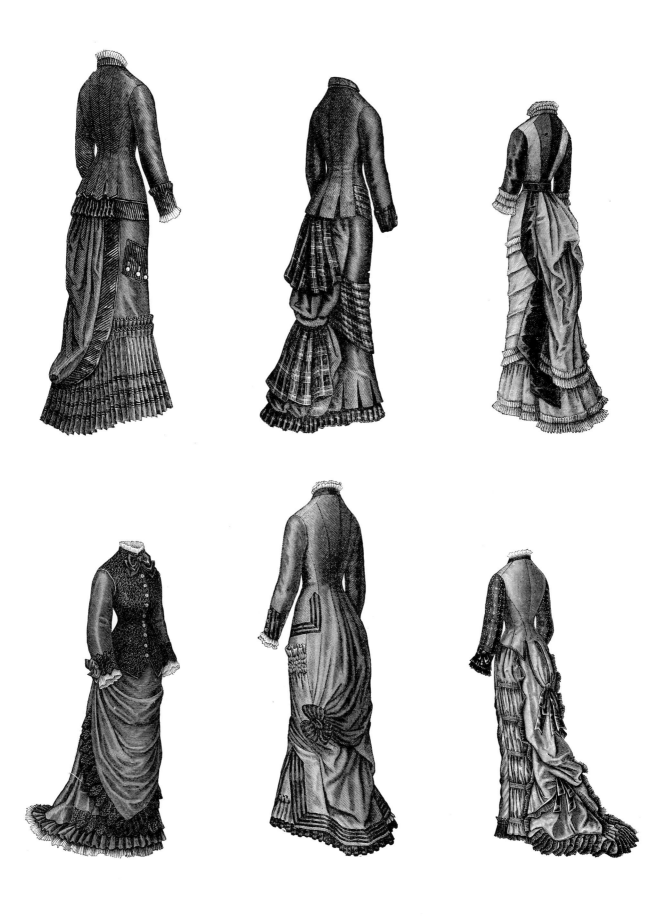

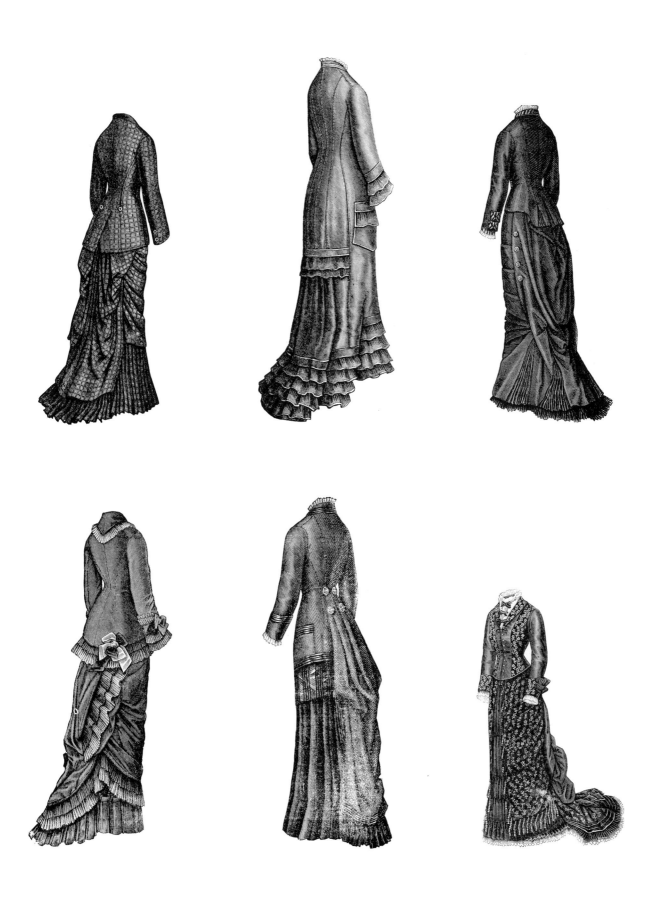

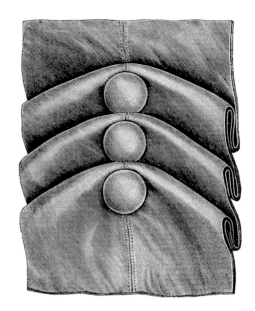

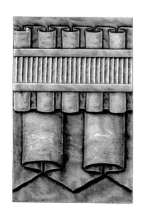

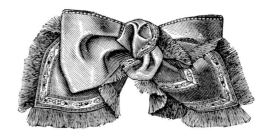

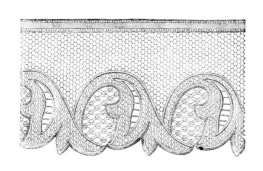

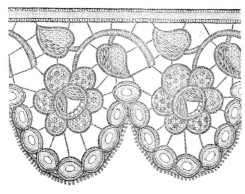

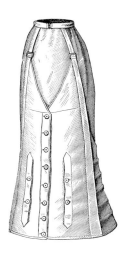

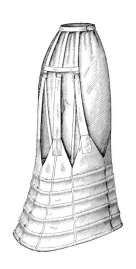

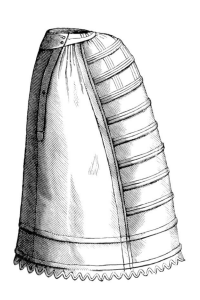

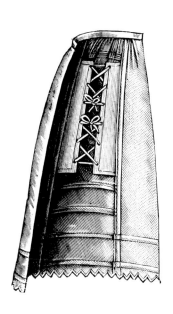

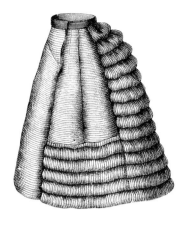

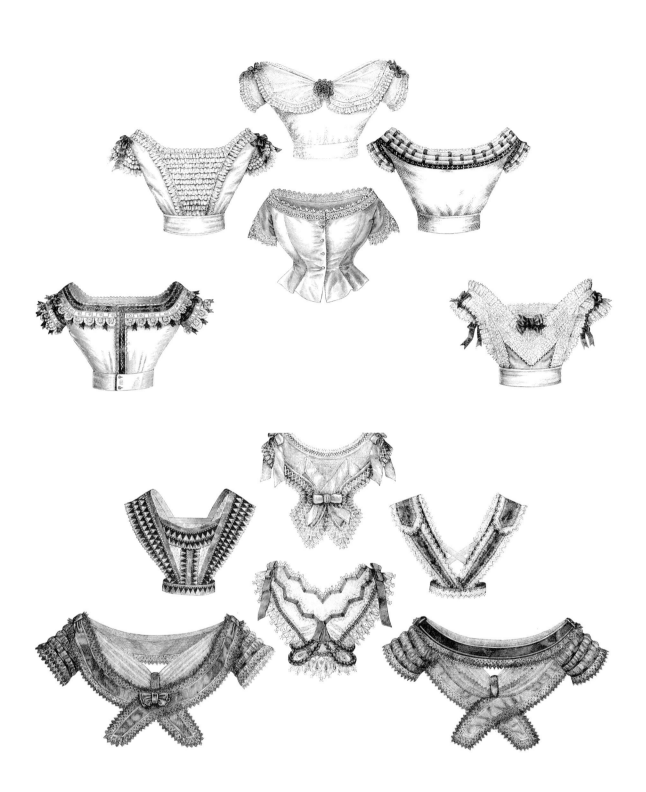

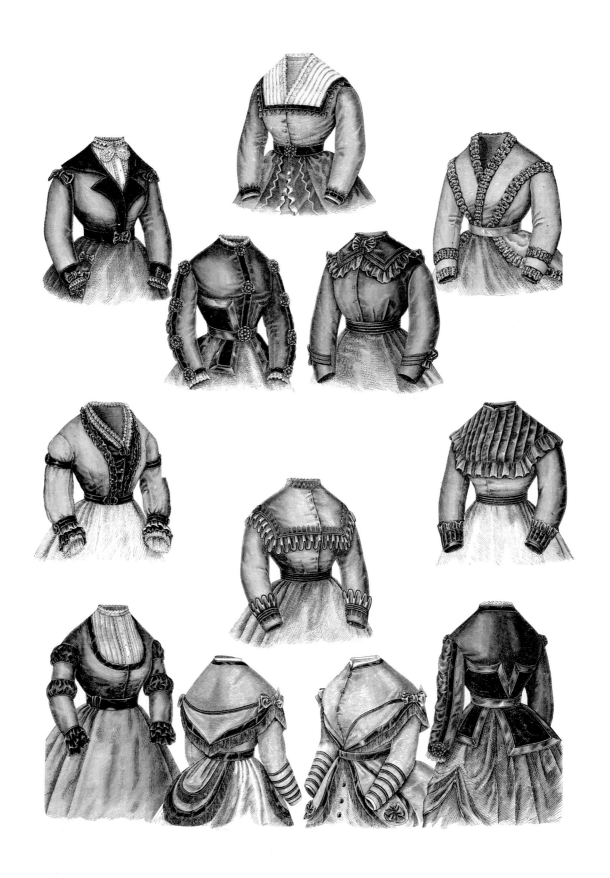

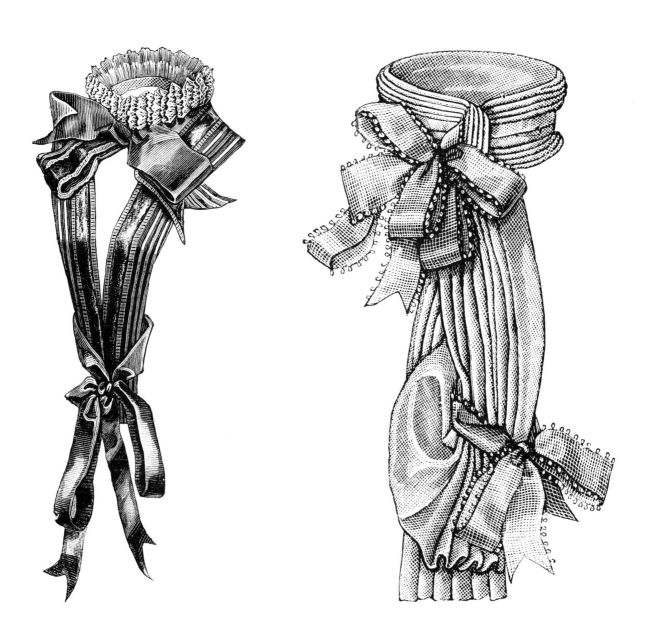

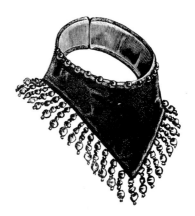

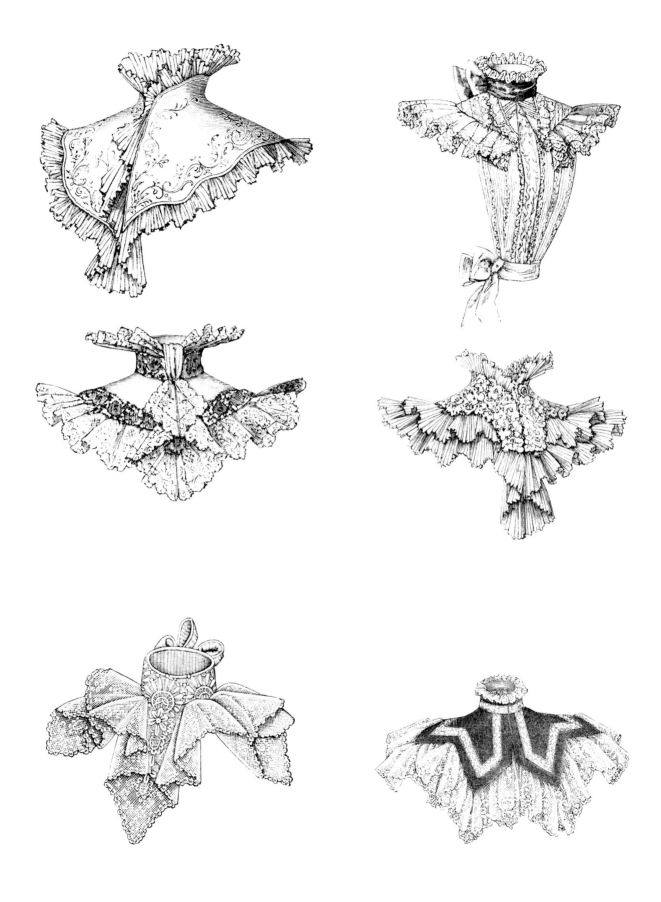

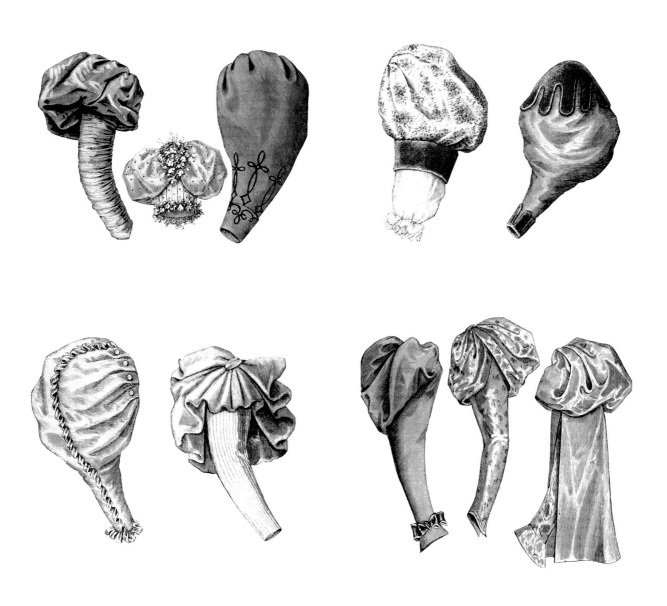

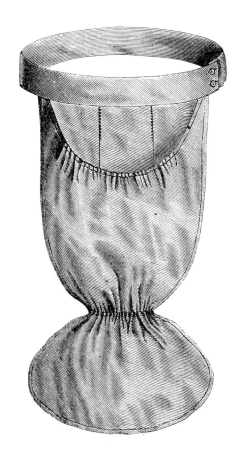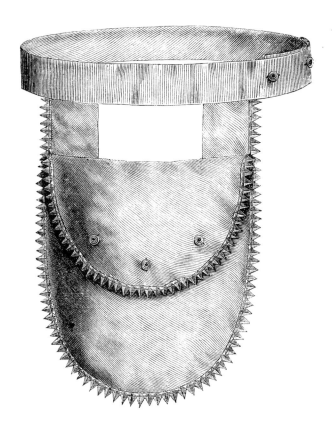

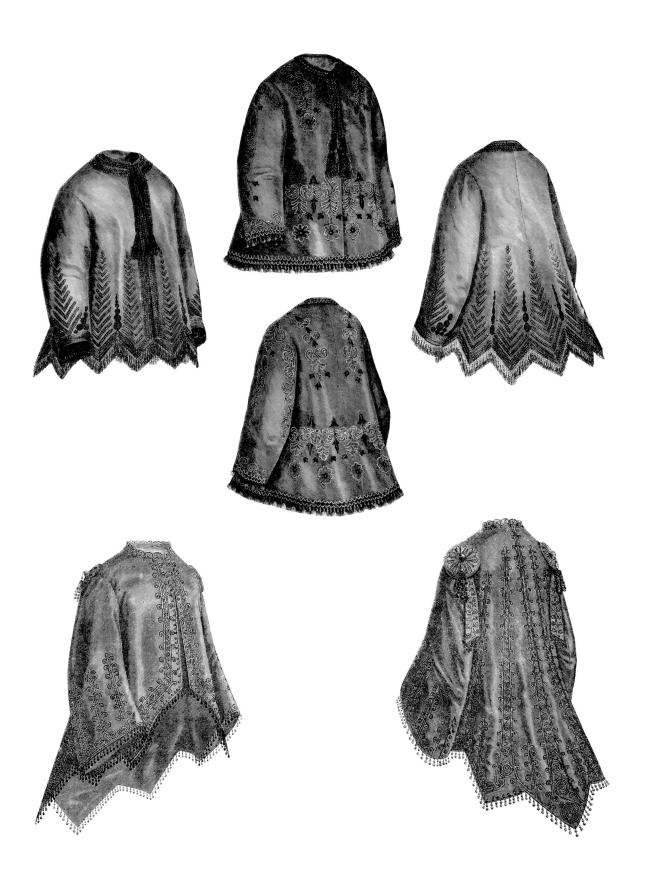

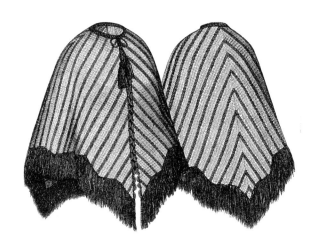

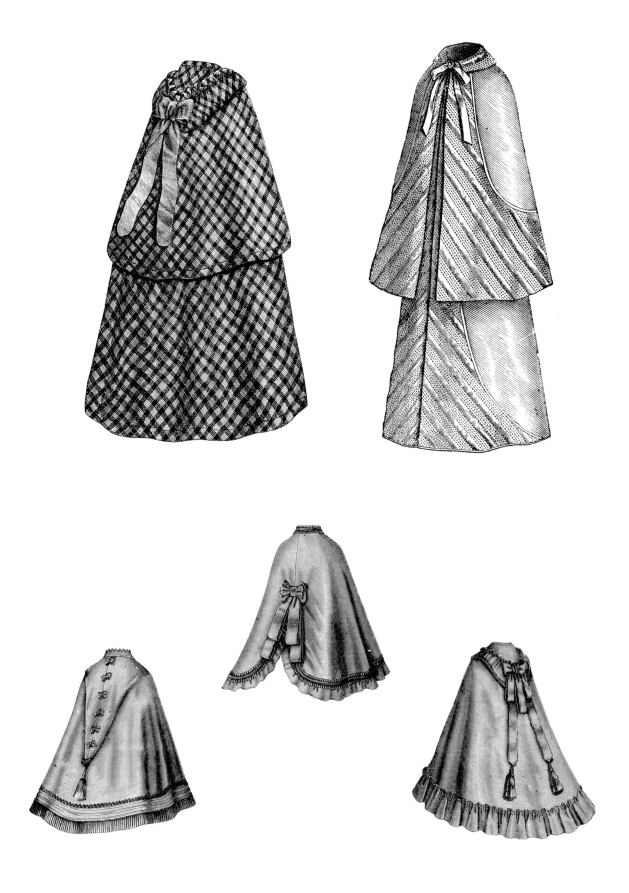

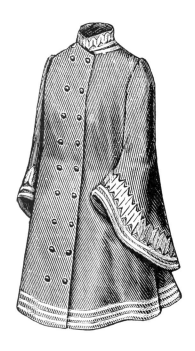

151

153

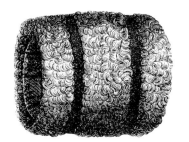 

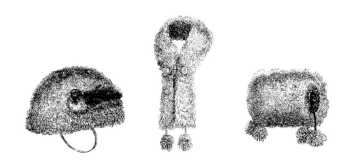

184

211

222

257

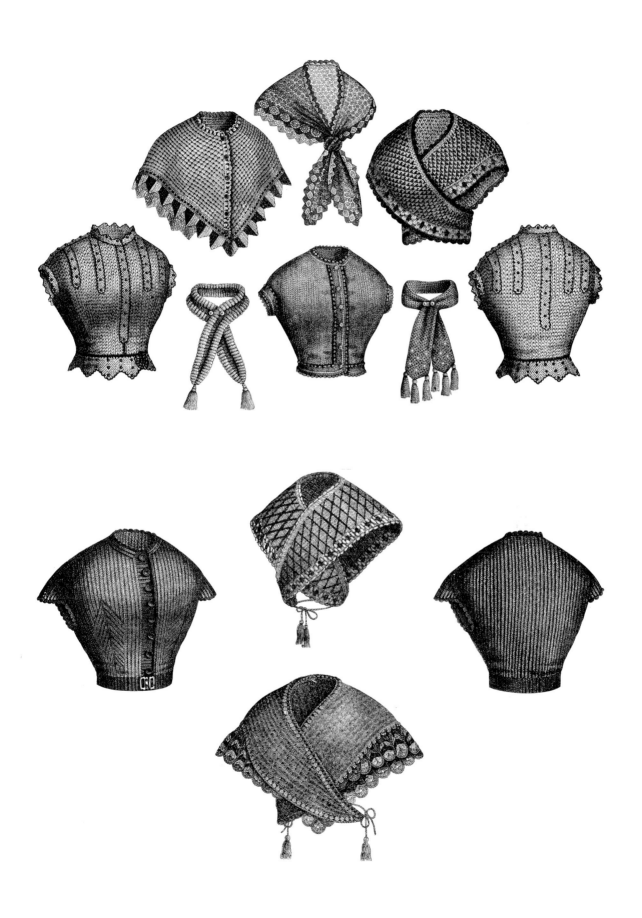

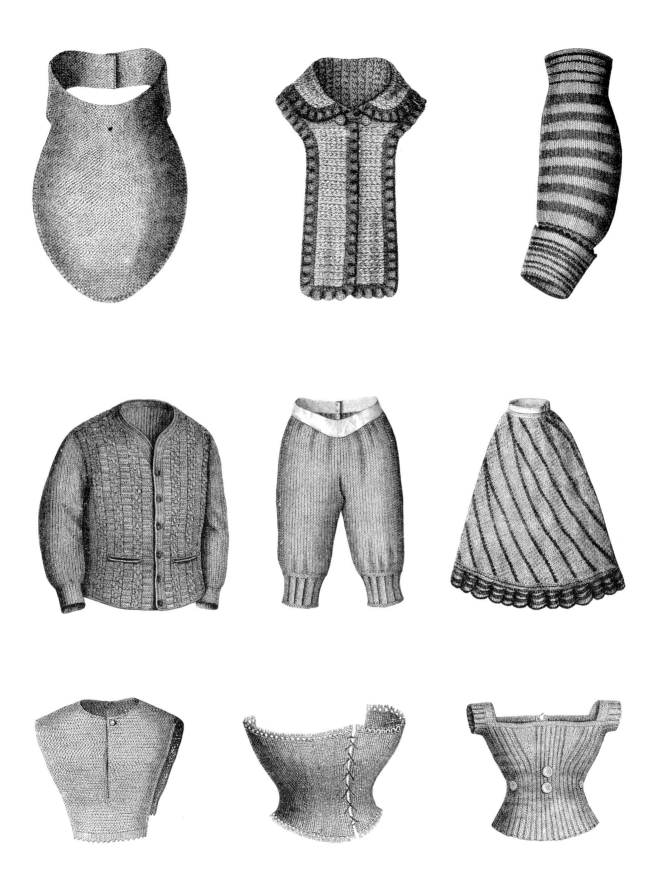

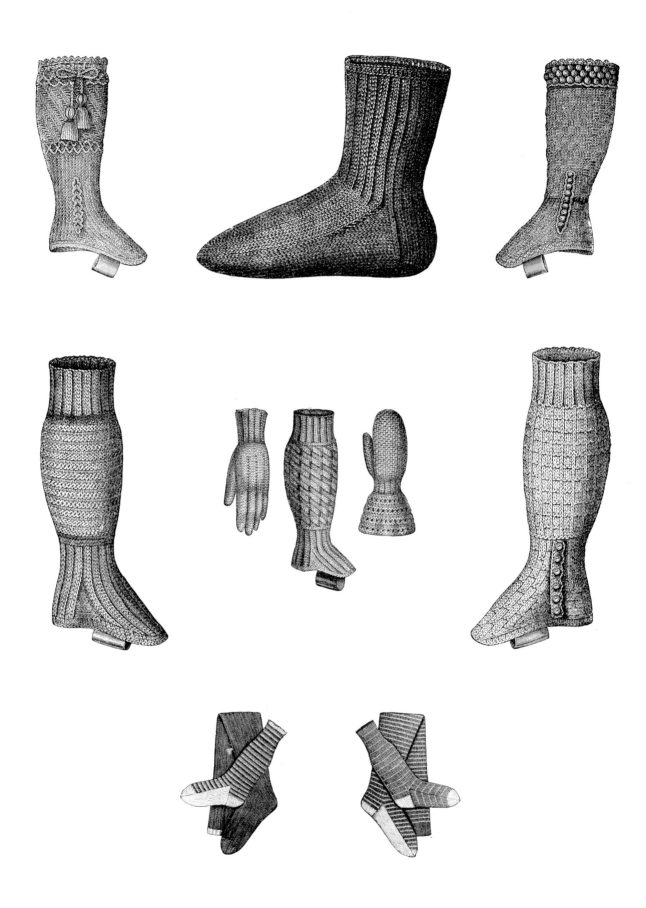

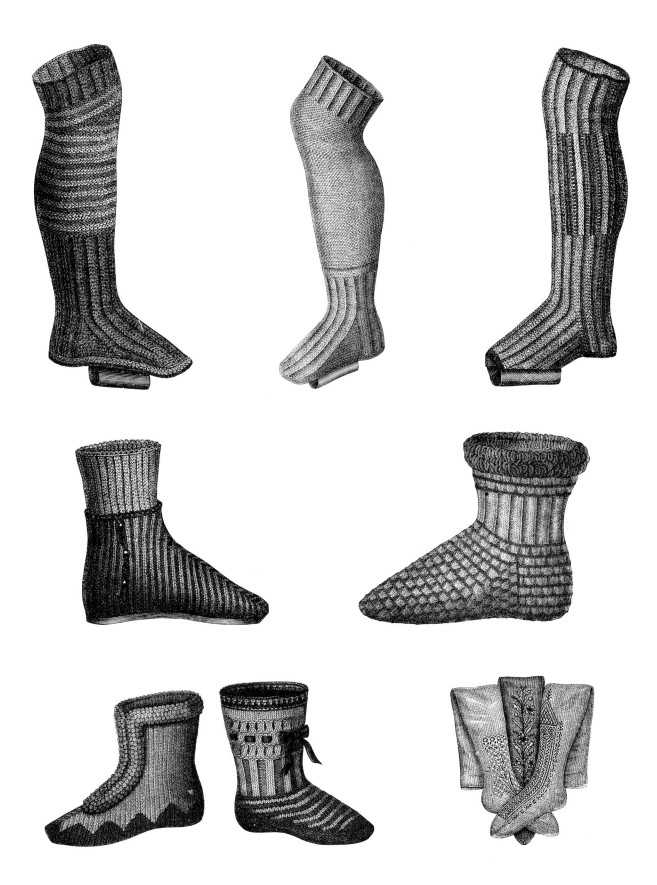

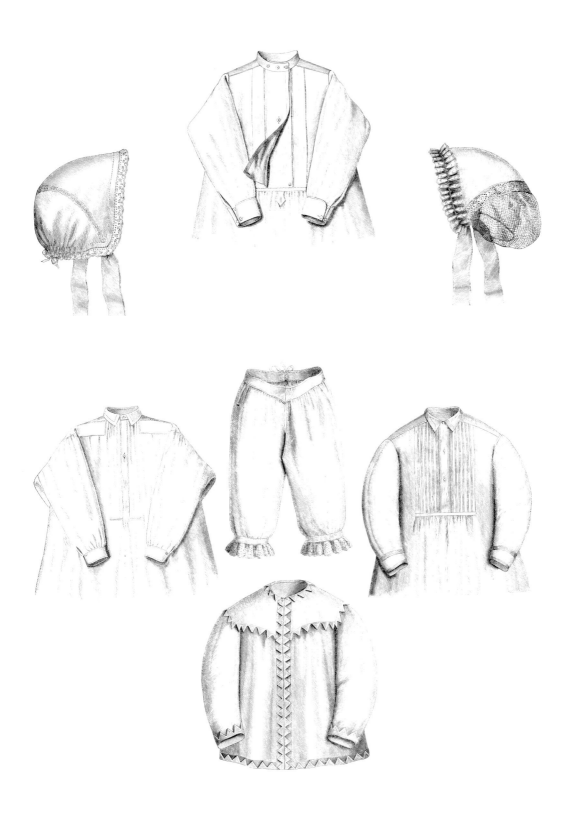

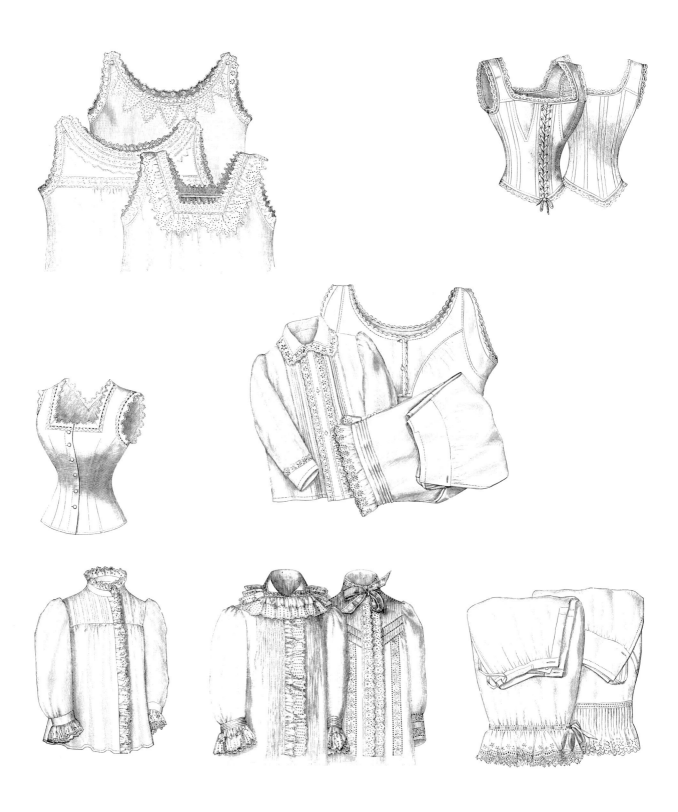

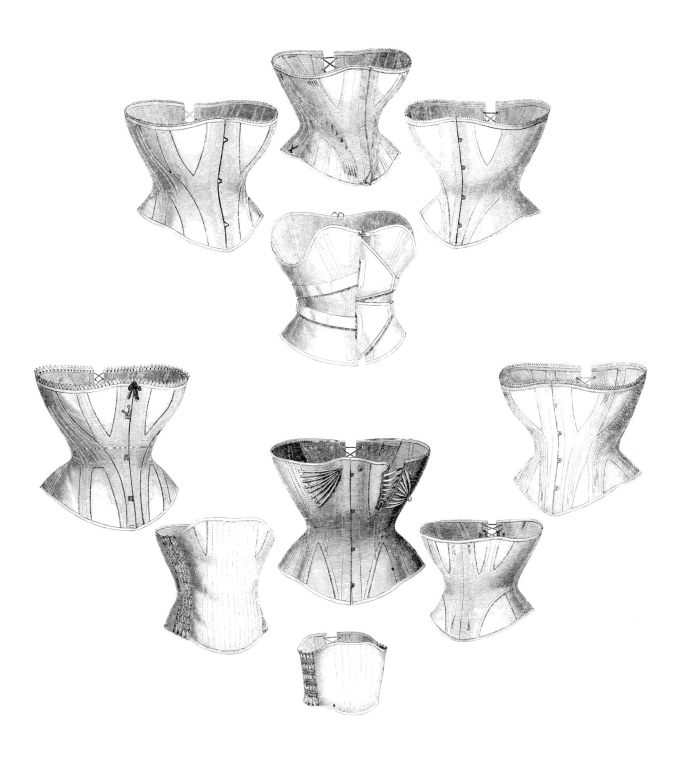

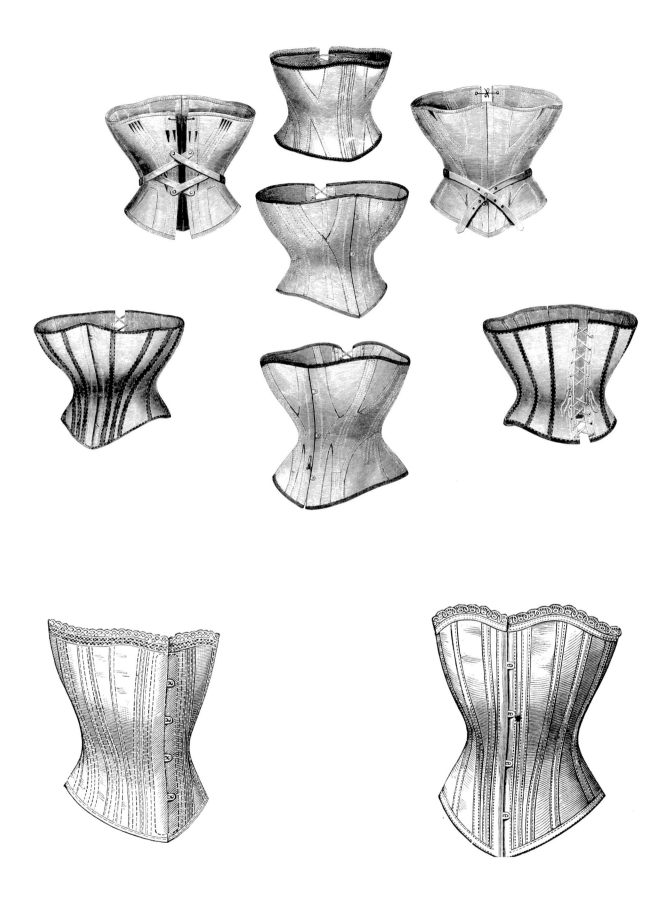

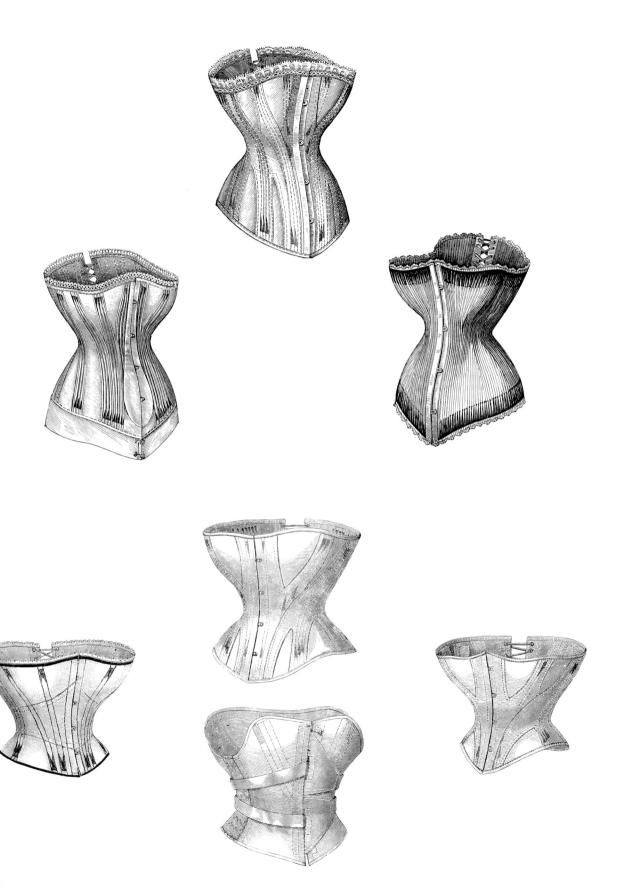

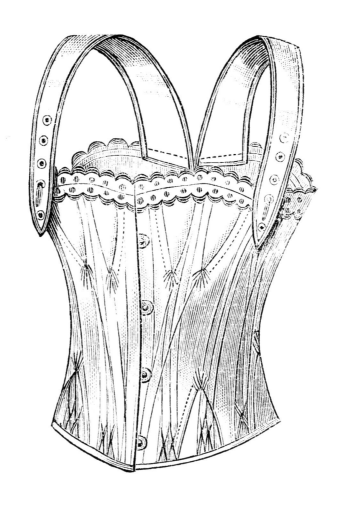

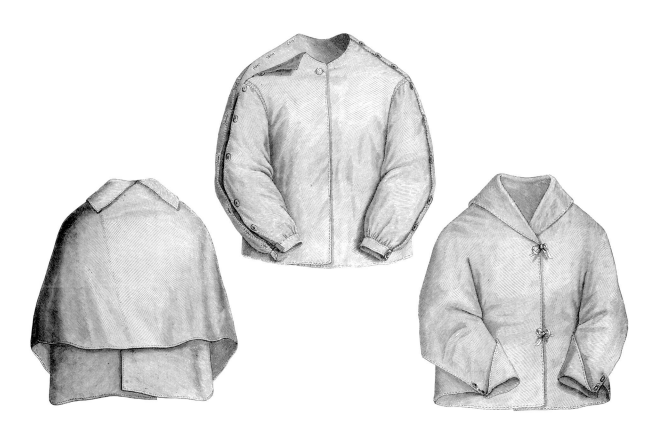

306

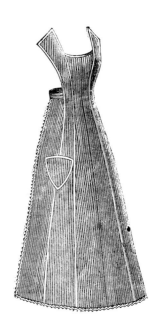

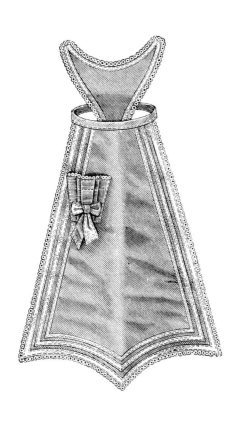

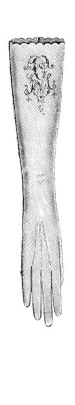
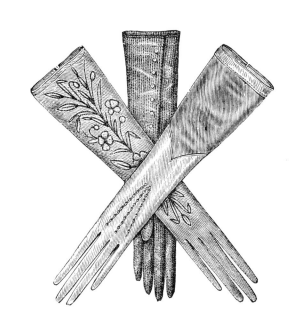

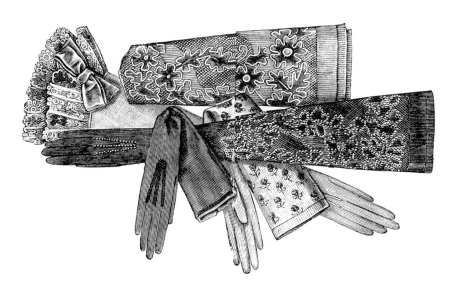

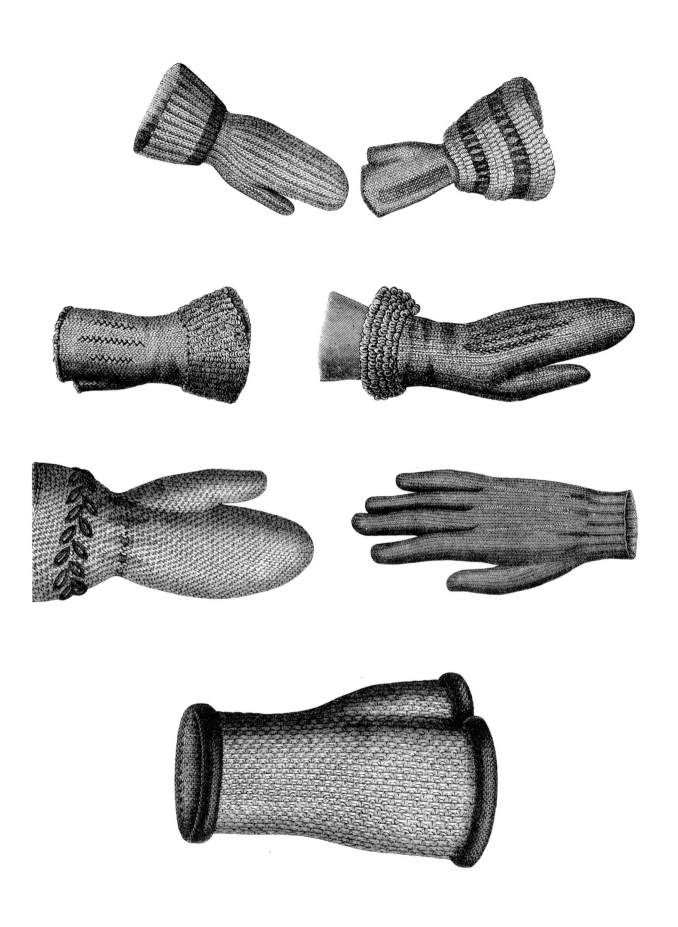

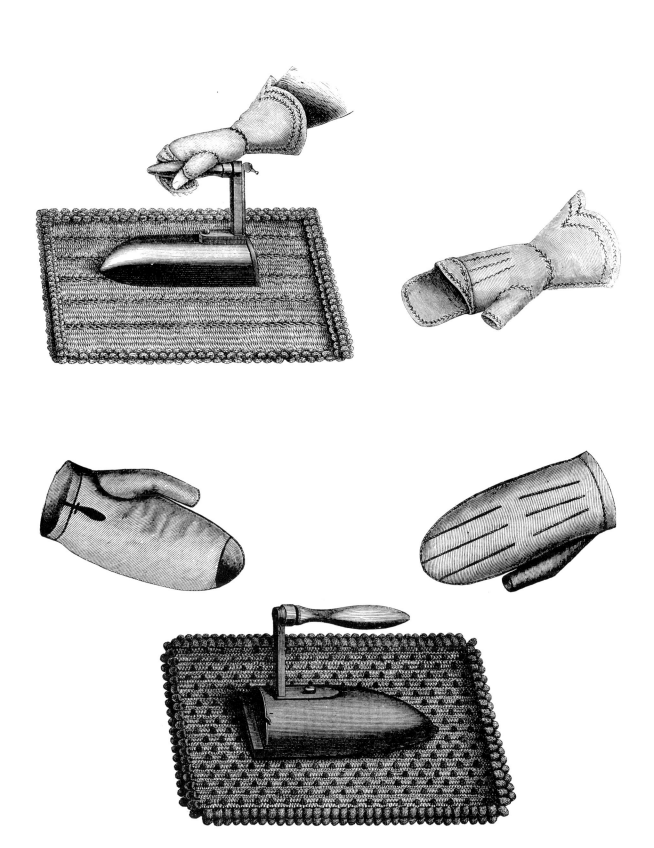

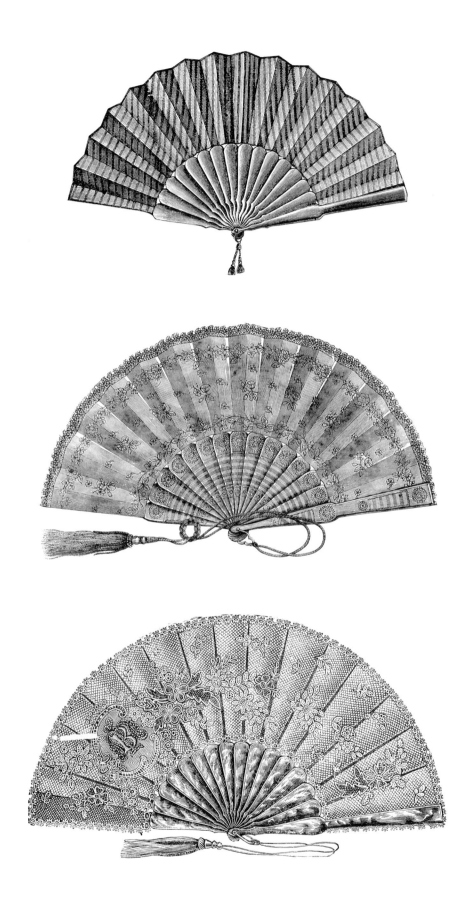

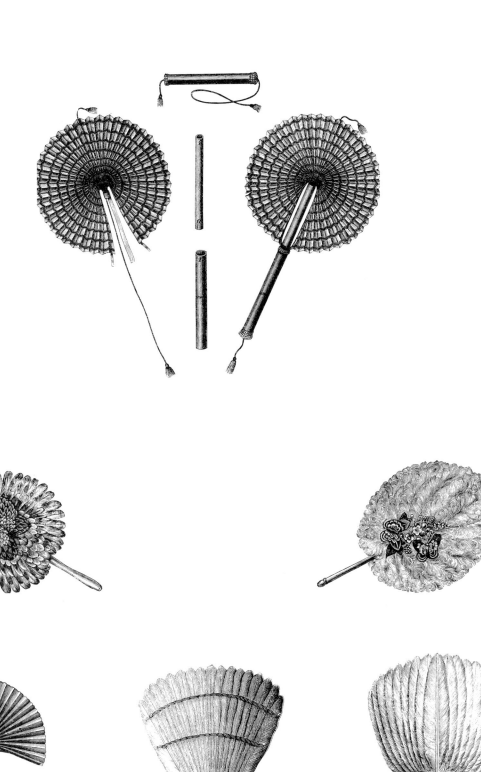

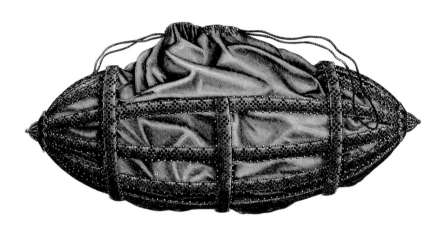

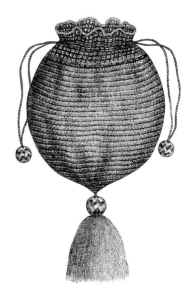

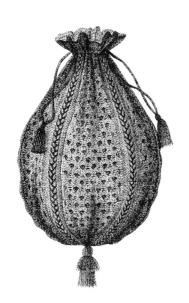

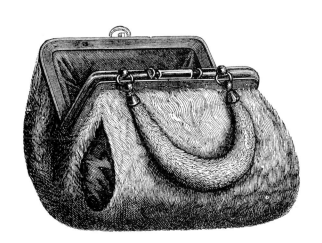

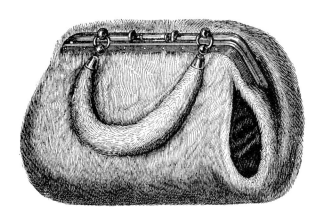

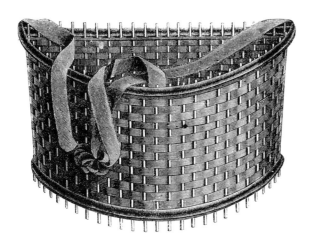

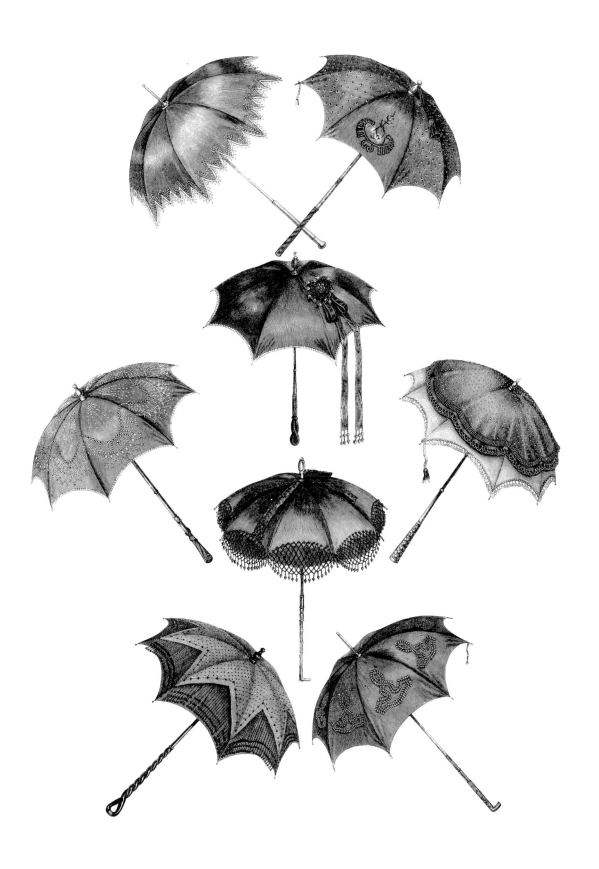

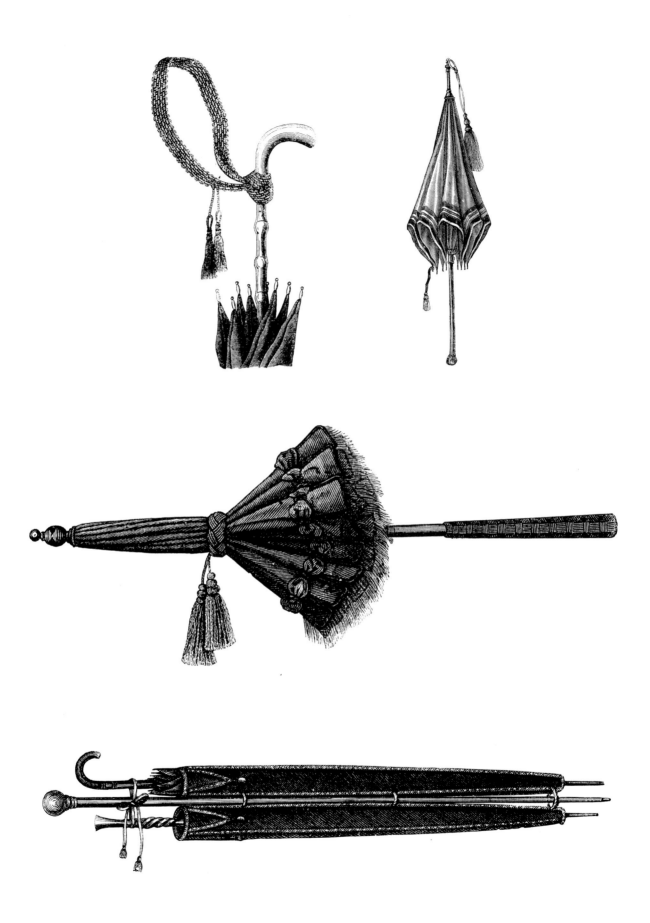

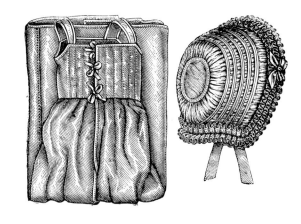

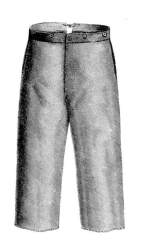

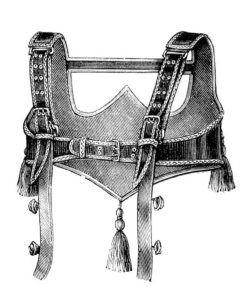

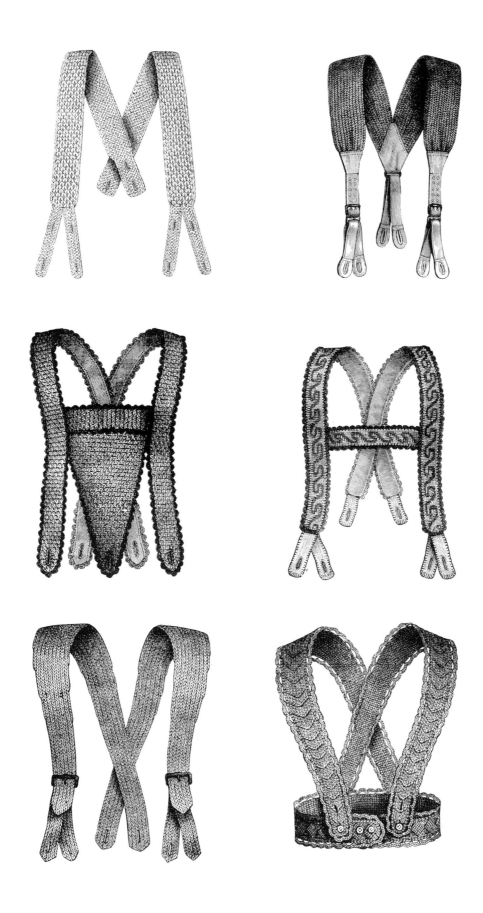

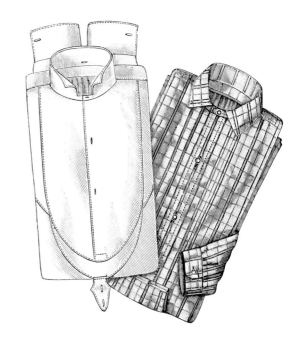

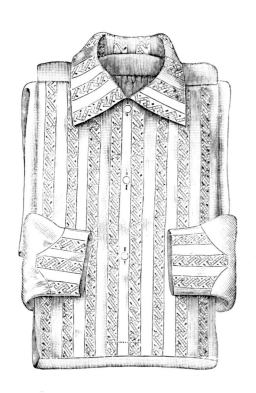

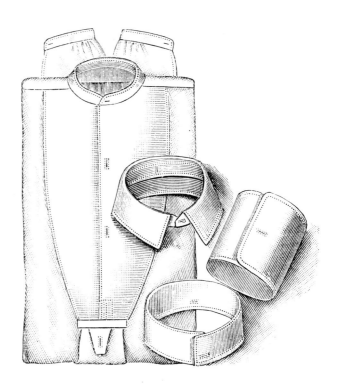

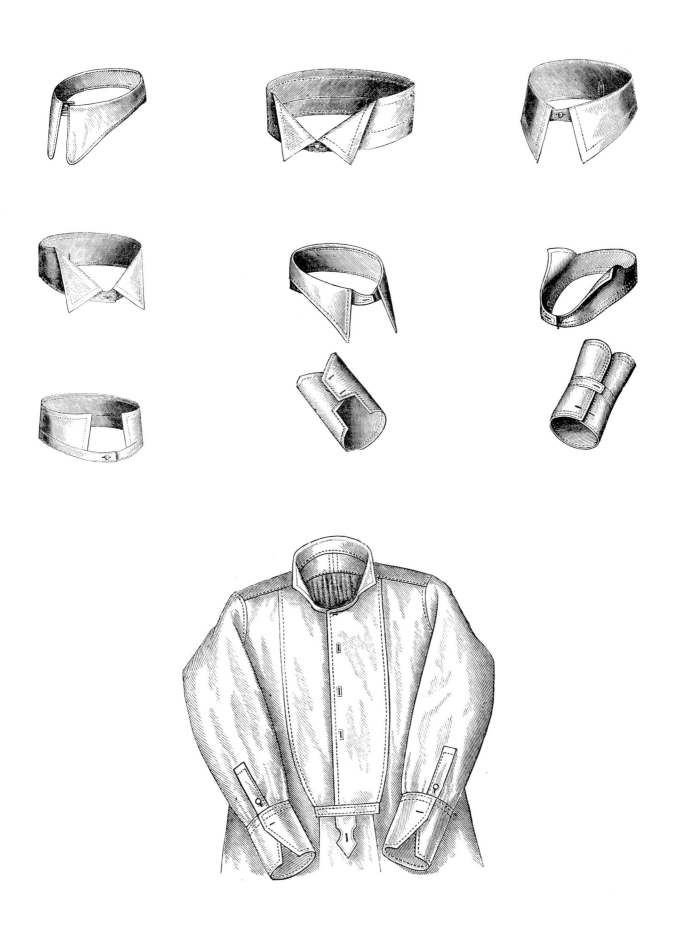

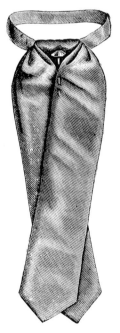

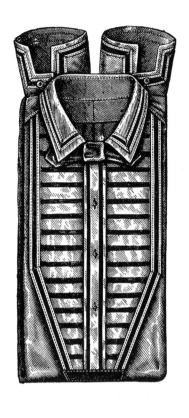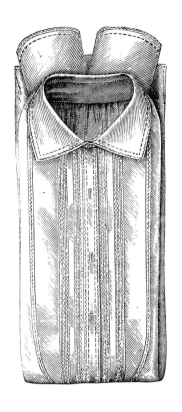

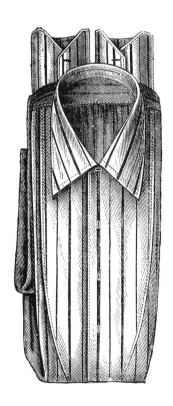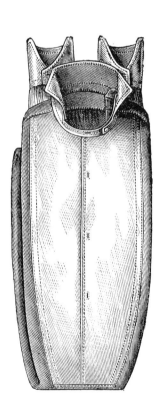